BIBLE QUIZZ

FOR ALL OC

VERNON HOWARD

First published 1947
Reprinted 1949, 1955, 1957,
1961, 1964, 1968,
1971, 1974, 1978, 1980

ISBN 0 7208 0019 6
Cat. No. 01/0204

 Printed in Great Britain for Pickering & Inglis Ltd, 26 Bothwell Street, Glasgow G2 6PA by Lowe & Brydone Printers Limited, Thetford, Norfolk.

Contents

GENERAL QUIZ

1. Do we read about Dorcas in the Old or the New Testament?
2. Who said, "What I have written I have written"?
3. What two Old Testament books begin with the letter L?
4. Is the city of Corinth in Italy or Greece?
5. What is a denarius?
6. For what is Nimrod famous?
7. Is William Carey famous as a missionary, a preacher, or a hymn writer?
8. Is Hebron a lake, an island, or a city?
9. Which is the correct number of years of Methuselah's life—473, 792, or 969?
10. What Bible character do you associate with a burning bush?
11. The fatted calf was killed for whom?
12. Is mustard mentioned in the Bible?
13. Name a well-known Bible animal with just two letters in its name.
14. Who was the "beloved physician"?
15. Whose name is generally associated with that of Balak?

Answers

1. New Testament.
2. Pilate.
3. Leviticus, Lamentations.
4. Greece.
5. A Coin.
6. As a "mighty hunter."
7. A Missionary.
8. A City.
9. 969.
10. Moses.
11. Prodigal Son.
12. Yes, several times.
13. Ox.
14. Luke.

15. Balaam.

True or False?

1. Spain is not mentioned in the Bible.
2. The book of Acts was written by Luke.
3. Felix was an Egyptian farmer.
4. The book of Jude contains only one chapter.
5. The Protestant Reformation successfully spread to Sweden.
6. Paul was a well educated man at the time of his conversion.
7. We read about the witch of Endor in the New Testament.
8. Luke was not one of the twelve disciples.
9. The book of Revelation deals largely with prophecy.
10. The name of Job's wife is not given in the Bible.
11. The story of Balak and Balaam is found in the New Testament.
12. Athens was not founded until fifty years after the birth of Christ.
13. The crime of Ananias and Sapphira was dishonesty.
14. Ham and Seth were brothers.
15. Noah's Ark came to rest upon Mount Ararat.

Yes or No?

Do any of the Bible books begin with the following letters? Quickly, now!

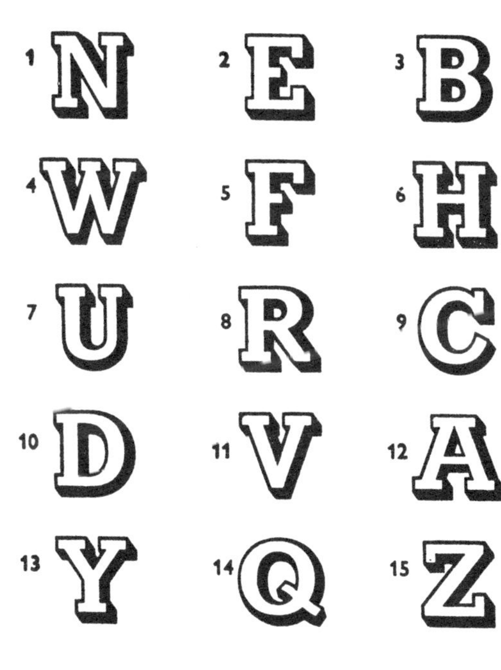

ANSWERS

1. Yes.	6. Yes.	11. No.
2. Yes.	7. No.	12. Yes.
3. No.	8. Yes.	13. No.
4. No.	9. Yes.	14. No.
5. No.	10. Yes.	15. Yes.

Letters in their names

Name at least four Bible characters with the following number of letters in their names.

1. 3
2. 4
3. 5
4. 6
5. 7
6. 8
7. 9

Answers

1. Lot, Job, Eve, Ham.
2. Paul, Adam, Ruth, Luke.
3. James, David, Jacob, Jonah, Moses.
4. Esther, Joseph, Elijah, Daniel.
5. Timothy, Deborah, Solomon, Matthew.
6. Jonathan, Jeremiah, Barnabas, Nehemiah.
7. Cornelius, Demetrius, Zephaniah, Zechariah.

TAKE YOUR ? CHOICE

1. The apostle Paul was born in Athens, Tarsus, Samaria.
2. Cornelius was a Roman, Egyptian, Greek.
3. The book that follows Isaiah is Jonah, Psalms, Jeremiah.
4. Job's "friends" numbered three, seven, ten.
5. The city of Alexandria is in Italy, Assyria, Egypt.
6. The mother of Ishmael was Miriam, Hagar, Deborah.
7. Joseph's Egyptian master was Potiphar, Ephraim, Laban.
8. The story of Samson and Delilah is found in Genesis, Leviticus, Judges.
9. Ebal is the name of a mountain, sea, river.
10. John Wyclif was a missionary, orphanage founder, reformer.

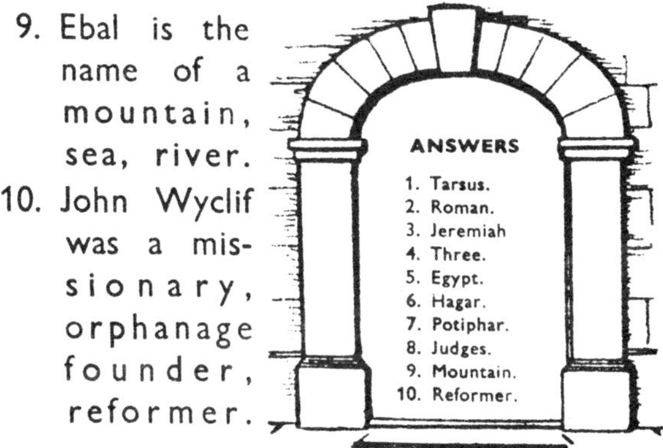

FATHERS AND SONS

CAN you name the fathers of these Bible men?

1. - - - - - Joshua
2. - - - - - Abraham
3. - - - - - David
4. - - - - - James
5. - - - - - Japheth
6. - - - - - Solomon
7. - - - - - Isaac
8. - - - - - Seth
9. - - - - - Jacob
10. - - - - - Samuel
11. - - - - - Joseph
12. - - - - - Jonathan

Answers

1. Nun.
2. Terah.
3. Jesse.
4. Zebedee.
5. Noah.
6. David.
7. Abraham.
8. Adam.
9. Isaac.
10. Elkanah.
11. Jacob.
12. Saul.

BOOKS and EVENTS

IN which Bible book do we read about each event? They are all found in the Old Testament.

1. The speech of Eliphaz.
2. The ten plagues.
3. The dethronement of Queen Vashti.
4. The birth of Samuel.
5. The death of Sarah.
6. Nebuchadnezzar's dream.
7. The fall of Jericho.
8. The marriage of Boaz.
9. Rebuilding the wall of Jerusalem.
10. A famous preaching mission to Nineveh.

ANSWERS

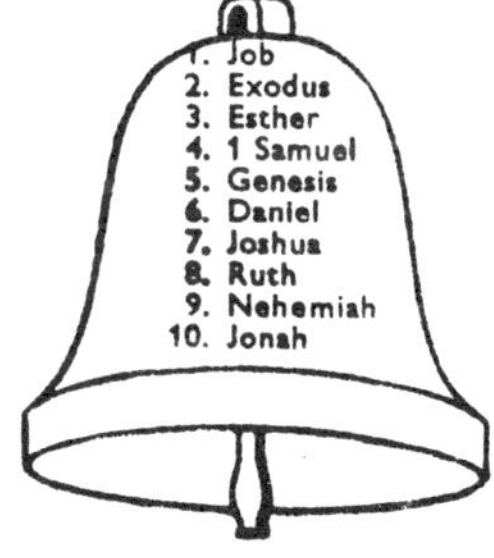

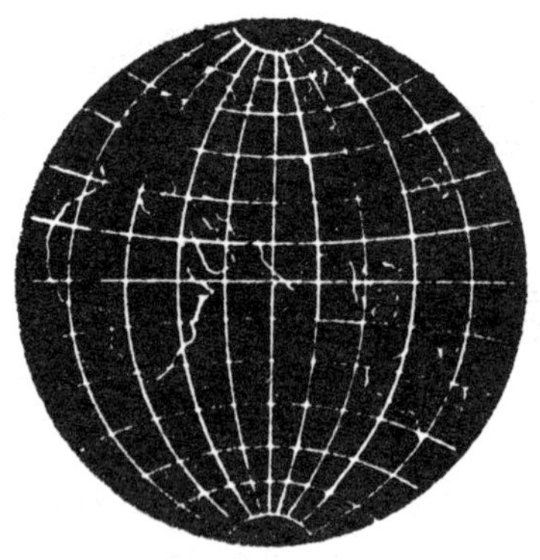

GREAT MISSIONARIES

HOW many first names can you supply to this list of famous missionaries?

1. .... Judson
2. .... Mackay
3. .... Moffat
4. .... Carey
5. .... Taylor
6. .... Paton
7. .... Martyn
8. .... Slessor
9. .... Livingstone
10. .... Morrison

ANSWERS

1 Adoniram 6 John G.
2 Alexander 7 Henry
3 Robert 8 Mary
4 William 9 David
5 J. Hudson 10 Robert

COMPLETE the following familiar Bible verses.

1. "Blessed are they that mourn: . . .
2. "Let the words of my mouth, and the meditation of my heart . . .
3. "Greater love hath no man than this, . . .
4. "Be not overcome of evil, . . .
5. "Boast not thyself of to-morrow; . . .
6. "God is our refuge and strength, . . .
7. "I have fought a good fight, I have finished my course, . . .
8. "A soft answer turneth away wrath: . . .
9. "Great peace have they which love Thy law: . . .
10. "If ye shall ask anything in My name, . . .

ANSWERS

1. . . . for they shall be comforted" (Matthew 5. 4).
2. . . . be acceptable in Thy sight, O Lord, my strength and my Redeemer" (Psalm 19. 14).
3. . . . that a man lay down his life for his friends" (John 15. 13).
4. . . . but overcome evil with good" (Romans 12. 21).
5. . . . for thou knowest not what a day may bring forth" (Proverbs 27. 1).
6. . . . a very present help in trouble" (Psalm 46. 1).
7. . . . I have kept the faith" (2 Timothy 4. 7).
8. . . . but grievous words stir up anger" (Proverbs 15. 1).
9. . . . and nothing shall offend them" (Psalm 119. 165).
10. . . . I will do it" (John 14. 14).

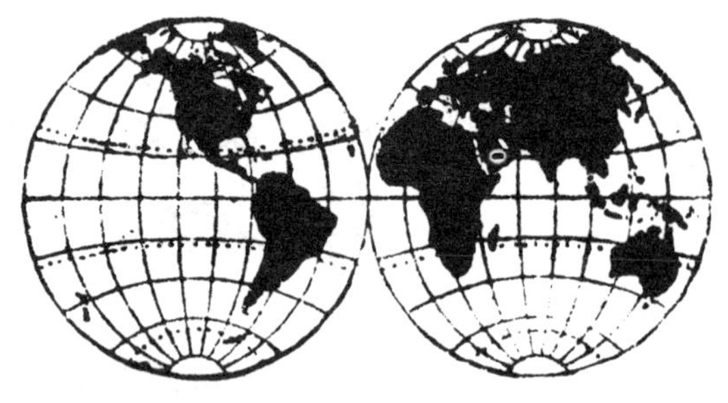

CITIES AND COUNTRIES

In what Bible-mentioned countries are the following modern cities located?

1. NAPLES
2. ADDIS ABABA
3. ALEXANDRIA
4. ATHENS
5. MEDINA
6. BARCELONA
7. CALCUTTA
8. TEHRAN
9. JERUSALEM
10. ANKARA

1. Where in the Bible do we find the story of Paul's conversion?
2. With whom do you associate the miracle of staying the sun and the moon?
3. Which is the only New Testament book which is classified as prophecy?
4. Is Portugal mentioned in the Bible?
5. What were the occupations of the two men whose dreams were interpreted by Joseph while in prison?
6. What was the surname of the disciple Judas?
7. Were Philip and Andrew brothers?
8. Which disciple doubted that his Lord was alive?
9. What Old Testament book follows the Psalms?
10. Is Nebo an island, a mountain, or a garden?
11. Name at least two of Paul's companions on his missionary journeys.
12. Were Ruth and David related?
13. Are foxes mentioned in the Bible?
14. In the New Testament, who was the seller of purple?
15. What famous hymn did Henry Francis Lyte write?

ANSWERS

1. The Book of Acts.
2. Joshua.
3. Revelation.
4. No.
5. Baker, Butler.
6. Iscariot.
7. No.
8. Thomas.
9. Proverbs.
10. A Mountain.
11. Barnabas and Silas.
12. Yes, Ruth was David's great grandmother.
13. Yes.
14. Lydia.
15. Abide with Me.

Wives and Husbands

CAN you supply the names of the husbands of the following Bible women?

1. Ruth.
2. Sapphira.
3. Sarah.
4. Hannah.
5. Asenath.
6. Esther.
7. Elisabeth.
8. Rebekah.
9. Priscilla.
10. Michal.
11. Zipporah.
12. Jezebel.
13. Leah.
14. Drusilla.
15. Bernice.

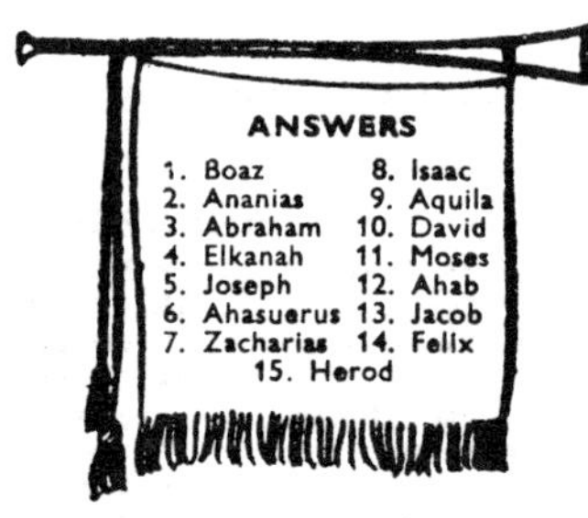

WHAT Bible books come immediately before and after the following New Testament books?

1. MARK.
2. TITUS.
3. EPHESIANS.
4. JAMES.
5. JUDE.
6. ACTS.
7. JOHN.
8. PHILEMON.
9. PHILIPPIANS.
10. 3 JOHN.

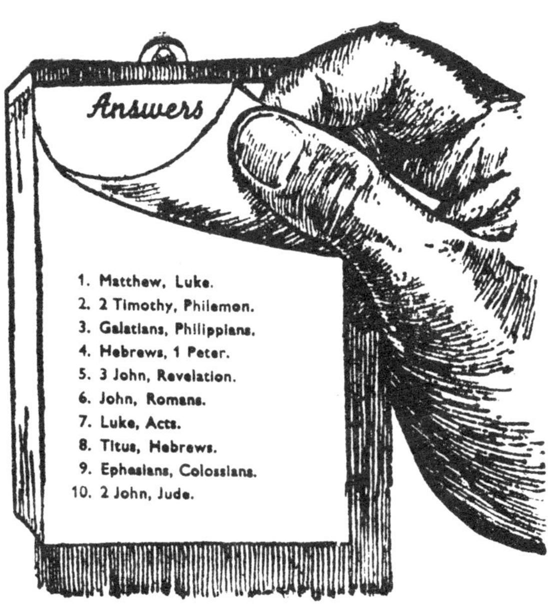

Unfinished Verses

1. "Surely goodness and mercy shall follow me all the days of my life: . . .
2. "For the wages of sin is death; . . .
3. "Open Thou mine eyes, . . .
4. "For there is one God, . . .
5. "Thy word have I hid in mine heart, . . .
6. "Fear not, little flock; . . .
7. "For other foundation can no man lay than that is laid, . . .
8. "Therefore being justified by faith, . . .
9. "Blessed are they which are persecuted for righteousness' sake: . . .
10. "Come now, and let us reason together, saith the Lord: . . .

Answers

1. . . . and I will dwell in the house of the Lord for ever." (Psalm 23. 6).
2. . . . but the gift of God is eternal life through Jesus Christ our Lord" (Romans 6. 23).
3. . . . that I may behold wondrous things out of Thy law" (Psalm 119. 18).
4. . . . and one mediator between God and men, the man Christ Jesus" (1 Timothy 2. 5).
5. . . . that I might not sin against Thee" (Psalm 119. 11).
6. . . . for it is your Father's good pleasure to give you the kingdom" (Luke 12. 32).
7. . . . which is Jesus Christ" (1 Corinthians 3. 11).
8. . . . we have peace with God through our Lord Jesus Christ" (Rom. 5. 1)
9. . . . for their's is the kingdom of heaven" (Matthew 5. 10).
10. . . . though your sins be as scarlet, they shall be as white as snow; though they be red like crimson, they shall be as wool" (Isaiah 1. 18).

CHRISTIAN OR NON-CHRISTIAN

ARE the following countries of the world principally Christian? Yes or no?

1. ARABIA.
2. ICELAND.
3. INDIA.
4. CHINA.
5. CANADA.
6. BELGIAN CONGO.
7. TURKEY.
8. ALASKA.
9. AFGHANISTAN.
10. BURMA.
11. AUSTRALIA.
12. BORNEO.
13. GREENLAND.
14. NEWFOUNDLAND
15. TIBET.
16. EGYPT
17. THAILAND.
18. LABRADOR.
19. LIBYA.
20. NEW ZEALAND.

GENERAL QUIZ

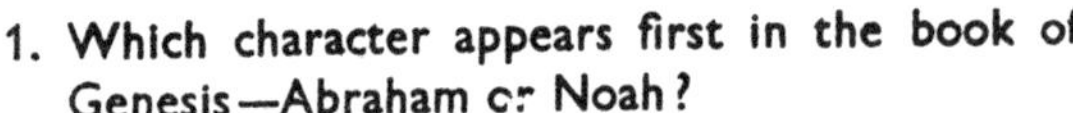

1. Which character appears first in the book of Genesis—Abraham or Noah?
2. Who was Bartimæus?
3. Where do we find the ten commandments?
4. Is Easter mentioned in the Bible?
5. Is Morocco principally a Christian country?
6. What is another name for the Lake of Gennesareth?
7. Which book occurs first—Esther or Psalms?
8. How many books are there in the entire Bible?
9. Name at least three Bible countries that begin with the letter A.
10. What was the Sanhedrin?
11. Were sundials used in Bible days?
12. What was meant by usury in Bible times?
13. What large island in the Mediterranean Sea near Italy was visited by Paul?
14. What does the word Genesis mean?
15. Did Cleopatra live before or after Christ?

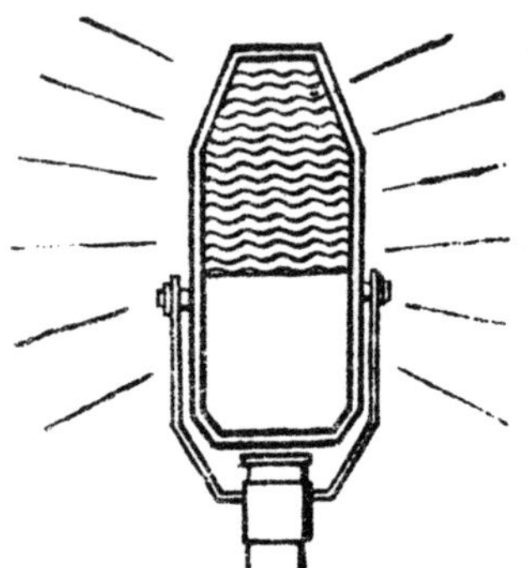

ANSWERS

1. Noah.
2. A beggar whom Jesus healed of blindness.
3. Exodus 20 and Deuteronomy 5.
4. Yes, in Acts 12. 4.
5. No.
6. Sea of Galilee.
7. Esther.
8. Sixty-six.
9. Arabia, Armenia, Assyria.
10. The Jewish Supreme Council.
11. Yes.
12. Interest on loaned money.
13. Sicily—see Acts 28. 12.
14. Origin or beginning.
15. Before.

NAME the one character in each group who is out of place. This means that the remaining two will have something in common.

1. Ruth, Nehemiah, Boaz.
2. Silas, Paul, Lazarus.
3. Japheth, Seth, Shem.
4. Felix, Bildad, Job.
5. Andrew, Titus, Bartholomew
6. Luke, Mark, Nicodemus.
7. Esther, Haman, Saul.
8. Lot, Abraham, Jonathan.
9. Samson, Benjamin, Joseph.
10. Daniel, Herod, Nebuchadnezzar.

ANSWERS

1. Which book has the most chapters?
2. How many books did James write?
3. Which is the last book of the Bible?
4. Who wrote the first five books of the Bible?
5. What are the first four books of the New Testament called?
6. Which comes first—Nehemiah or Judges?
7. Which is the shortest Bible book?
8. Did Thomas write any Bible books?
9. Which is the last book of the Old Testament?
10. Does the book of Ruth have four or twenty chapters?

ANSWERS

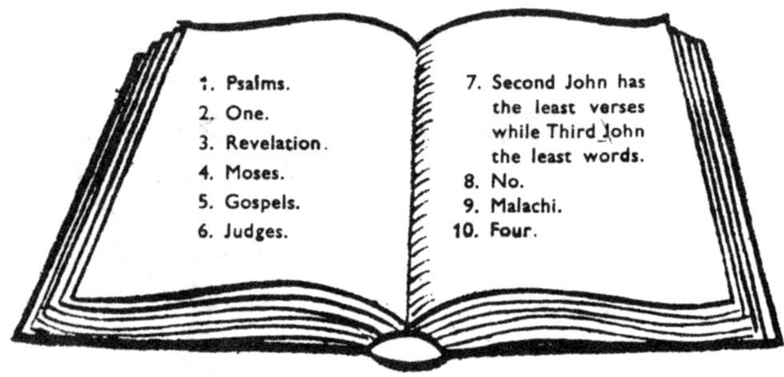

True or False?

1. Jerusalem is within a mile of the Sea of Galilee.
2. The name "Richard" is not mentioned in the Bible.
3. Soap was unknown in Bible days.
4. The book of Proverbs occurs before Daniel.
5. Mary Slessor was a noted missionary to Africa.
6. Paul was a Roman citizen.
7. The city of Samaria is in Egypt.
8. The cormorant is a type of bird.
9. The story of David and Goliath is found in the book of Genesis.
10. To journey from Egypt to Palestine you would go north-east.
11. Agrippa is the name of a New Testament king.
12. The book of James follows the book of Hebrews.
13. Lot's wife was named Abigail.
14. Alexander Mackay was a famous Christian business man.
15. Belshazzar was the king who saw the hand writing on the wall.

? RELATIVES ?

WHAT was the relationship between the following couples?

1. MARTHA and LAZARUS.
2. LOIS and EUNICE.
3. ABRAHAM and LOT.
4. JUDAH and DINAH.
5. ISAAC and JOSEPH.
6. RUTH and ORPAH.
7. LEAH and RACHEL.
8. ESAU and ABRAHAM.
9. MOSES and MIRIAM.
10. EVE and SETH.

ANSWERS

1. Sister—Brother.
2. Mother—Daughter.
3. Uncle—Nephew.
4. Brother—Sister
5. Grandfather—Grandson.
6. Sisters-in-law.
7. Sisters.
8. Grandson—Grandfather.
9. Brother—Sister.
10. Mother—Son.

SCRAMBLED NEW TESTAMENT BOOKS

Can you identify them?

1 RAKM.
2. ELEVRNOITA.
3. RASONM.
4. BEHWESR.
5. SCAT.
6. LIHPENOM.
7. ITSUT.
8. EJDU.
9. MAJSE.
10. KELU.

R
S

1. Mark
2. Revelation
3. Romans
4. Hebrews
5. Acts
6. Philemon
7. Titus
8. Jude
9. James
10. Luke

First Letters

Here is another quiz that calls for quick answers. You must name three Bible characters whose names begin with each of the following letters. Only ten seconds for each set!

1 S	2 H	3 A
4 M	5 E	6 L
7 D	8 N	9 B
10 R	11 P	12 C
13 G	14 I	15 J
16 T	17 O	18 Z

ANSWERS

1. Samuel, Solomon, Shem.
2. Hannah, Herod, Ham.
3. Aaron, Andrew, Adam.
4. Mark, Matthew, Martha.
5. Eve, Elijah, Esau.
6. Lot, Luke, Levi.
7. David, Dorcas, Daniel.
8. Naomi, Nathan, Nehemiah.
9. Benjamin, Barnabas, Boaz.
10. Ruth, Reuben, Rachel.
11. Philip, Paul, Peter.
12. Caleb, Cain, Cornelius.
13. Gideon, Goliath, Gad.
14. Isaac, Ishmael, Isaiah.
15. James, John, Jacob.
16. Timothy, Titus, Terah.
17. Obadiah, Obed, Orpah.
18. Zacchaeus, Zephaniah, Zechariah

First Words of Bible Verses

CAN you quote at least one Bible verse that begins with each following word?

1. "For . . . .
2. "And . . . .
3. "Now . . . .
4. "He . . . .
5. "Be. . . . .
6. "If . . . .
7. "In . . . .
8. "A . . . .
9. "We . . . .
10. "Do . . . .
11. "Love . . . .
12. "But . . . .
13. "Let . . . .
14. "Come . . . .
15. "The. . . . .
16. "All . . . .
17. "Trust . . . .
18. "I . . . .
19. "Blessed . . . . . .
20. "Beloved, ...

ANSWERS:

1. "For the Son of man is come to seek and to save that which was lost" (Luke 19. 10).
2. "And now abideth faith, hope, charity, these three; but the greatest of these is charity" (1 Cor. 13. 13).
3. "Now faith is the substance of things hoped for, the evidence of things not seen" (Hebrews 11. 1).
4. "He maketh me to lie down in green pastures; He leadeth me beside the still waters" (Psalm 23. 2).
5. "Be not overcome of evil, but overcome evil with good" (Romans 12. 21).
6. "If ye love Me, keep My commandments" (John 14. 15).
7. "In the beginning God created the heaven and the earth" (Genesis 1. 1.)
8. "A soft answer turneth away wrath: but grievous words stir up anger" (Proverbs 15. 1).
9. "We love Him, because He first loved us" (1 John 4. 19)
10. "Do all things without murmurings and disputings" (Philippians 2. 14).
11. "Love worketh no ill to his neighbour: therefore love is the fulfilling of the law" (Romans 13. 10).
12. "But God commendeth His love toward us, in that, while we were yet sinners, Christ died for us" (Romans 5. 8).
13. "Let the words of my mouth, and the meditation of my heart, be acceptable in Thy sight, O Lord, my strength and my Redeemer" (Psalm 19. 14).
14. "Come unto Me, all ye that labour and are heavy laden, and I will give you rest" (Matthew 11. 28).
15. "The Lord is my Shepherd; I shall not want" (Psalm 23. 1).
16. "All things were made by Him; and without Him was not anything made that was made" (John 1. 3).
17. "Trust in the Lord with all thine heart; and lean not unto thine own understanding" (Proverbs 3. 5).
18. "I am the true vine, and My Father is the husbandman" (John 15. 1).
19. "Blessed are the merciful: for they shall obtain mercy" (Matthew 5. 7).
20. "Beloved, if God so loved us, we ought also to love one another" (1 John 4. 11).

? ? ? ? ? ? ? ? ? ? ? ? ? ? ?

WHO CAME FIRST ?

If we started at Genesis and read through the Bible, which of the following Bible folks would we read about first?

1. Esther or Ruth?
2. Seth or Shem?
3. Isaac or Benjamin?
4. Sarah or Delilah?
5. Mary or Sapphira?
6. John or Pilate?
7. John the Baptist or Luke
8. Andrew or Cornelius?
9. David or Aaron?
10. Moses or Jonathan?
11. Paul or Herod?
12. James or Luke?
13. Timothy or Matthew?
14. Noah or Samson?
15. Abraham or Joseph?
16. Thomas or Stephen?
17. Solomon or Joshua?
18. Miriam or Rachel?
19. Jonah or Daniel?
20. Job or Jacob?

Answers

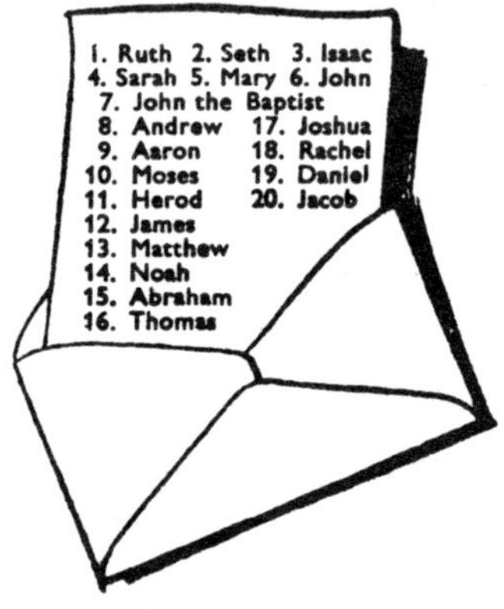
1. Ruth 2. Seth 3. Isaac
4. Sarah 5. Mary 6. John
7. John the Baptist
8. Andrew
9. Aaron
10. Moses
11. Herod
12. James
13. Matthew
14. Noah
15. Abraham
16. Thomas
17. Joshua
18. Rachel
19. Daniel
20. Jacob

TRUE OR FALSE?

1. The Lord Jesus was about thirty years old when He began His ministry.
2. John was called the "beloved disciple."
3. After the death of Moses, the Children of Israel were led by Aaron.
4. Paul was one of the original twelve disciples.
5. The Old Testament contains thirty-nine books.
6. Haman died of old age.
7. Joseph became the governor of Egypt.
8. The new Testament contains twenty-seven books.
9. We read about Rhoda in the Old Testament.
10. Crete is an island in the Mediterranean Sea.
11. King Agrippa appears in the Old Testament.
12. The book of Titus was written by Paul.
13. The Sea of Galilee is larger than the Mediterranean Sea.
14. Matthew was an Ethiopian.
15. David wrote the twenty-third Psalm.

ANSWERS

General Quiz

1. Which is the only New Testament book which is classified as history?
2. Name a Bible character whose name begins with the letter V.
3. Would you say that the entire Bible contains 334,286 words or 773,692 words?
4. Who was Bildad?
5. In Bible days, what was a tetrarch?
6. Who asked, "Sirs, what must I do to be saved?"
7. Name a well-known Bible king with fourteen letters in his name.
8. Which Old Testament book is longer—Genesis or Jonah?
9. What direction would you travel in order to go from Palestine to Greece?
10. Name the three sons of Noah.
11. Name six of Jacob's twelve sons.
12. Was Peter married?
13. Who saw a ladder in a dream?
14. Name two famous brothers who wrote hundreds of hymns.
15. What is a Timbrel?

ANSWERS

1. Acts.
2. Vashti.
3. 773,692 words.
4. One of Job's "friends."
5. A Governor.
6. The Philippian Jailor.
7. Nebuchadnezzar.
8. Genesis.
9. Northwest.
10. Shem, Ham, Japheth.
11. Reuben, Levi, Judah, Joseph, Benjamin, Zebulun.
12. Yes.
13. Jacob.
14. Charles and John Wesley.
15. A Hebrew Musical Instrument.

SCRAMBLED OLD TESTAMENT BOOKS

Can you identify them?

1. HOJAN.
2. DOESUX.
3. THRU.
4. SAPLSM.
5. RAEZ.
6. SAIIHA.
7. OJLE.
8. SUHAJO.
9. MOSA.
10. ANDLIE.

Answers

5 BIBLE FIVES 5

Supply five answers for each subject.

1. CITIES.
2. COUNTRIES.
3. MOUNTAINS.
4. BIRDS.
5. ANIMALS.
6. DISCIPLES OF CHRIST.
7. SONS OF JACOB.
8. KINGS.
9. FOODS.
10. EPISTLES OF PAUL.

ANSWERS

1. Bethlehem, Jerusalem, Nazareth, Jericho, Rome.
2. Egypt, Italy, Greece, Ethiopia, Palestine.
3. Ararat, Nebo, Sinai, Hermon, Moriah.
4. Hawk, Owl, Sparrow, Eagle, Dove.
5. Lion, Bear, Horse, Sheep, Ox.
6. James, John, Thomas, Andrew, Philip.
7. Joseph, Benjamin, Judah, Reuben, Dan.
8. Herod, Saul, David, Solomon, Nebuchadnezzar.
9. Honey, Fish, Bread, Corn, Figs.
10. Galatians, Ephesians, Philippians, Colossians, Romans.

BEFORE AND AFTER

What Bible books come immediately before and after the following Old Testament books?

1. PROVERBS.
2. EXODUS.
3. RUTH.
4. DANIEL.
5. JOB.
6. ISAIAH.
7. JONAH.
8. NUMBERS.
9. ESTHER.
10. JUDGES.

ANSWERS

1. Psalms, Ecclesiastes.
2. Genesis, Leviticus.
3. Judges, 1 Samuel.
4. Ezekiel, Hosea.
5. Esther, Psalms.
6. Song of Solomon, Jeremiah.
7. Obadiah, Micah.
8. Leviticus, Deuteronomy.
9. Nehemiah, Job.
10. Joshua, Ruth.

ASSOCIATIONS

How quickly can you associate at least two Bible characters with the following?

1. A WELL.
2. CLOTHING.
3. MONEY.
4. FOOD.
5. PRISON.
6. A BOAT.
7. MUSIC.
8. A WALL.
9. A KINGDOM.
10. THE ARMY.

Answers

1. Jacob, the Samaritan Woman
2. Joseph, Elisha
3. Judas, Ananias
4. Elijah, Eve
5. Joseph, Paul
6. Peter, Andrew
7. David, Jubal
8. Nehemiah, Joshua
9. Herod, Caesar
10. Cornelius, Goliath

1. "But seek ye first the kingdom of God, and His righteousness; . . .
2. "The Lord is my Shepherd; . . .
3. "Blessed are the peacemakers: . . .
4. "For what shall it profit a man, . . .
5. "I can do all things through Christ . . .
6. "Let us hear the conclusion of the whole matter: . . .
7. "Prove all things; . . .
8. "He that saith he abideth in Him, . . .
9. "Marvel not that I said unto thee, . . .
10. "Be not deceived; God is not mocked:. . .

Answers

1. . . . and all these things shall be added unto you" (Matthew 6. 33).
2. . . . I shall not want" (Psalm 23. 1).
3. . . . for they shall be called the children of God" (Matthew 5. 9).
4. . . . if he shall gain the whole world, and lose his own soul?" (Mark 8. 36)
5. . . . which strengtheneth me" (Philippians 4. 13).
6. . . . fear God, and keep His commandments: for this is the whole duty of man" (Ecclesiastes 12. 13).
7. . . . hold fast that which is good" (1 Thessalonians 5. 21).
8. . . . ought himself also to walk, even as He walked" (1 John 2. 6).
9. . . . Ye must be born again" (John 3. 7).
10. . . . for whatsoever a man soweth, that shall he also reap (Galatians 6. 7).

Did they know each other?

Here is another quiz with a time-limit on the answers. Did the following Bible couples know each other? Allow just three seconds for each answer.

1. Saul and Jonathan.
2. Lois and Timothy.
3. Cain and Shem.
4. Herod and Paul.
5. Ruth and Esther.
6. Andrew and Bartholomew.
7. Job and Sarah.
8. Samuel and Saul.
9. Jesse and David.
10. Benjamin and Ham.
11. Moses and Joseph.
12. Aaron and Miriam.
13. Paul and Mark.
14. Rachel and Hannah.
15. Barnabas and Silas.
16. Reuben and Shem.
17. Naomi and Martha.
18. Lot and Abraham.
19. Elisabeth and Leah.
20. Matthew and Philip.

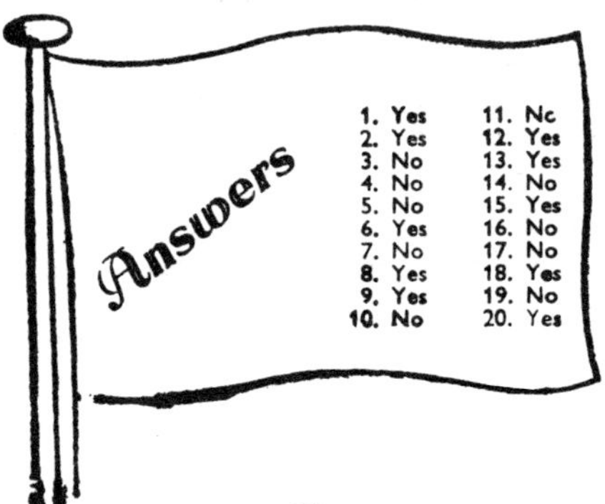

LETTERS and NAMES

HOW *quickly* can you name at least one Bible character whose name *ends* with the following letters?

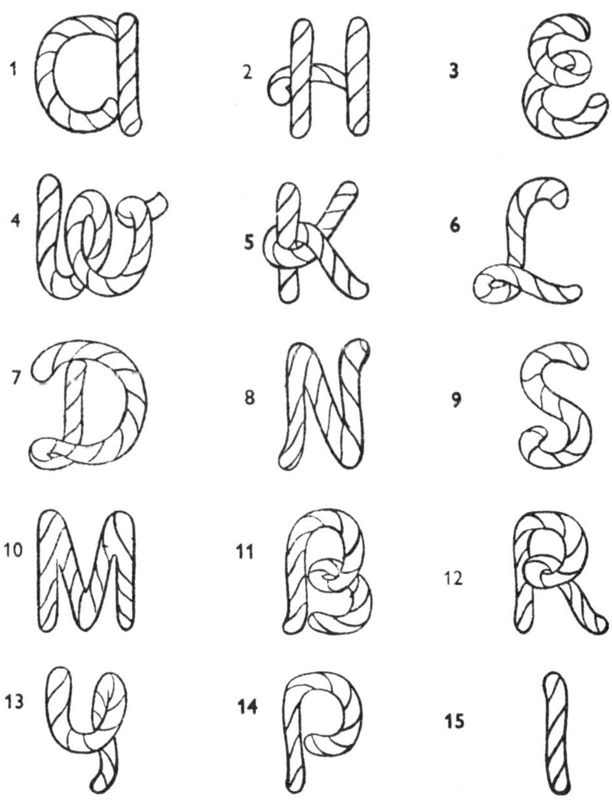

ANSWERS

1. Joshua.
2. Hannah.
3. Eve.
4. Andrew.
5. Mark.
6. Daniel.
7. David.
8. John.
9. Lois.
10. Adam.
11. Caleb.
12. Hagar.
13. Timothy.
14. Philip.
15. Levi.

1. "Yea, though I walk through the valley of the shadow of death, I will fear no evil: . . .
2. "Wherefore by their fruits . . .
3. "As newborn babes, desire the sincere milk of the Word, . . .
4. "Let not your heart be troubled: . . .
5. "Jesus saith unto him, I am the Way, the Truth, and the Life: . . .
6. "As far as the east is from the west, . . .
7. "Come unto Me, all ye that labour and are heavy laden, . . .
8. "But the fruit of the Spirit is . . .
9. "Blessed are they which do hunger and thirst after righteousness: . . .
10. "All Scripture is given by inspiration of God, . . .

1. . . . for Thou art with me; Thy rod and Thy staff they comfort me" (Psalm 23. 4).
2. . . . ye shall know them" (Matthew 7. 20).
3. . . . that ye may grow thereby" (1 Peter 2. 2).
4. . . . ye believe in God, believe also in Me" (John 14. 1).
5. . . . no man cometh unto the Father, but by Me" (John 14. 6).
6. . . . so far hath He removed our transgressions from us" (Psalm 103. 12).
7. . . . and I will give you rest" (Matthew 11. 28).
8. . . . love, joy, peace, longsuffering, gentleness, goodness, faith" (Gal. 5. 22).
9. . . . for they shall be filled" (Matthew 5. 6).
10. . . . and is profitable for doctrine, for reproof, for correction, for instruction in righteousness" (2 Timothy 3. 16).

BIBLE BROTHERS

Can you name at least one brother of the following characters?

1. ABEL.
2. ANDREW.
3. ESAU.
4. JAMES.
5. BENJAMIM.
6. SHEM.
7. JUDAH.
8. LEVI.
9. DAN.
10. AARON.

ANSWERS

Bible Names of Men

Here are ten sets of men's names. Which single name in each set is found in the Bible?

1.	ABNER,	ALFRED,	ALBERT.
2.	ROBERT,	FELIX,	CARL.
3.	WILLIAM,	MARVIN,	ALEXANDER.
4.	WALTER,	JASON,	RALPH.
5.	CLIFFORD,	CLAYTON,	LEMUEL.
6.	CHARLES,	EDWARD,	JOEL.
7.	IRA,	HERBERT,	GEORGE.
8.	OLIVER,	NATHAN,	EDMUND.
9.	EARL,	NICOLAS,	EDWIN.
10.	ROGER,	STUART,	CYRUS.

Answers

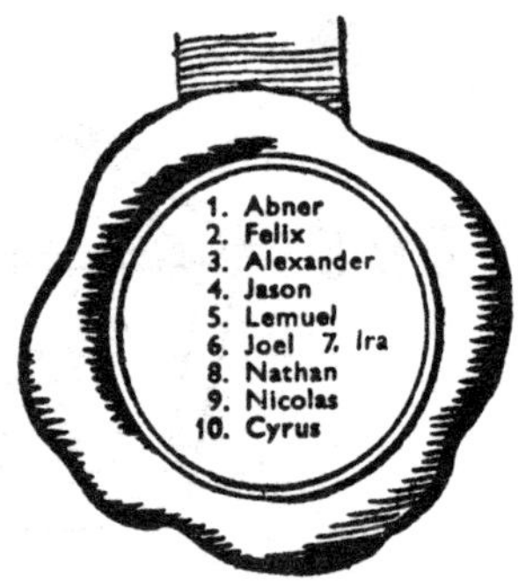

Unfinished Verses

1. "Thy word is a lamp unto my feet, . . .
2. "Therefore if any man be in Christ, he is a new creature: . . .
3. "He maketh me to lie down in green pastures:...
4. "Blessed are the pure in heart: . . .
5. "Trust in the Lord with all thine heart; . . .
6. "But my God shall supply all your need . . .
7. "Delight thyself also in the Lord; . . .
8. "Commit thy way unto the Lord; . . .
9. "Now faith is the substance of things hoped for, . . .
10. "Study to shew thyself approved unto God,. . .

Answers

1. . . . and a light unto my path" (Psalm 119. 105).
2. . . . old things are passed away; behold, all things are become new" (2 Corinthians 5. 17).
3. . . . He leadeth me beside the still waters" (Psalm 23. 2).
4. . . . for they shall see God" (Matthew 5. 8).
5. . . . and lean not unto thine own understanding" (Proverbs 3. 5).
6. . . . according to His riches in glory by Christ Jesus" (Philippians 4. 19)
7. . . . and He shall give thee the desires of thine heart" (Psalm 37. 4).
8. . . . trust also in Him; and He shall bring it to pass" (Psalm 37. 5).
9. . . . the evidence of things not seen" (Hebrews 11. 1).
10. . . . a workman that needeth not to be ashamed, rightly dividing the word of truth" (2 Timothy 2. 15).

GENERAL QUIZ ?

1. What is the last name of the famous hymn writer whose first names are Frances Ridley?
2. Where in the Bible do we find the story of Joseph?
3. Is Algeria principally a Christian country?
4. Was Dan a son of Jacob?
5. How many epistles did Peter write?
6. In what direction is Ethiopia from Egypt?
7. Name two sisters and a brother who lived in Bethany.
8. Is Moriah the name of a river or a mountain?
9. Was Thaddeus one of the twelve disciples?
10. What is the eighth book of the Old Testament?
11. Name the two Bible books that begin with the letter D.
12. Who said, "My punishment is greater than I can bear"?
13. Was David related to Jonathan?
14. Was Job a rich man or poor man when he died?
15. Do we read about Potiphar in connection with Moses or with Joseph?

ANSWERS

1. **Havergal**
2. **Genesis**
3. **No**
4. **Yes**
5. **Two**
6. **South**
7. **Mary, Martha, Lazarus**
8. **Mountain**
9. **Yes**
10. **Ruth**
11. **Deuteronomy Daniel**
12. **Cain**
13. **No**
14. **Rich man**
15. **Joseph**

True or False?

1. The next to last book of the New Testament is Jude.
2. The Mediterranean Sea was unknown in Old Testament days.
3. The verse, "Blessed are the pure in heart: for they shall see God," is found in the fifth chapter of Matthew.
4. Ruth was married to Boaz.
5. The book of Acts briefly mentions a visit by the apostle Paul to China.
6. The story of Joseph is found in Genesis.
7. Timothy wrote two of the New Testament books.
8. The book of Proverbs was written by Daniel.
9. Paul was a tent-maker by trade.
10. A scarlet gown was put on Jesus before His crucifixion.
11. Moses wrote the first five books of the Bible.
12. Honey was a well-known food in Bible days.
13. John Calvin was a leader of the Reformation in France.
14. We read about Haman in the story of Ruth.
15. The art of printing was unknown in Bible days.

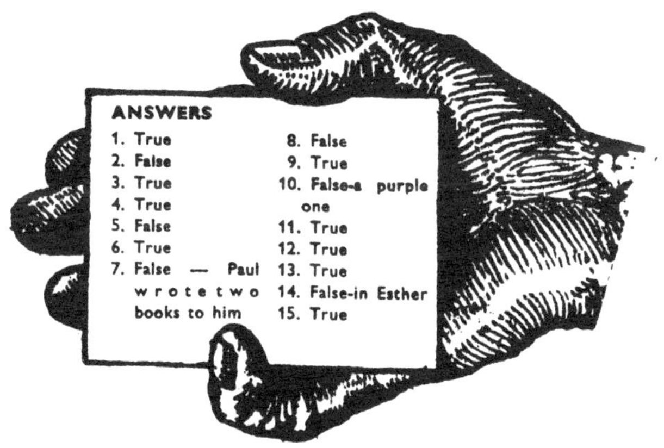

ANSWERS

1. True
2. False
3. True
4. True
5. False
6. True
7. False — Paul wrote two books to him
8. False
9. True
10. False-a purple one
11. True
12. True
13. True
14. False-in Esther
15. True

Old or New Testament?

This quiz calls for speed Do the following characters belong in the Old or New Testament? You are given just two seconds to answer.

1. CALEB.
2. AHAB.
3. JULIA.
4. DINAH.
5. FELIX.
6. PRISCILLA.
7. SILAS.
8. NATHAN.
9. LOIS.
10. JESSE.
11. POTIPHAR.
12. CORNELIUS.
13. HAMAN.
14. ENOCH.
15. CHLOE.
16. ZACCHÆUS
17. DORCAS.
18. HANNAH.
19. LEAH.
20. TITUS.

Answers

Bible Geography

In what direction would you travel in order to go from one of these Bible-mentioned places to the other?

1. From the Sea of Galilee to the Mediterranean Sea.
2. From Egypt to the Red Sea.
3. From Greece to Crete.
4. From the Mediterranean Sea to the River Jordan.
5. From Libya to Italy.
6. From Arabia to Egypt.
7. From Crete to Cyprus.
8. From Nazareth to Jerusalem.
9. From Palestine to Greece.
10. From Italy to Egypt.

ANSWERS

1. West.
2. East.
3. South-East.
4. East.
5. North.
6. West.
7. East
8. South.
9. North-West.
10. South-East.

Unfinished Verses

1. "Thou preparest a table before me in the presence of mine enemies: . . .
2. "For all have sinned, . . .
3. "This is a faithful saying, and worthy of all acceptation, . . .
4. "For God so loved the world, that He gave His only begotten Son, . . .
5. "In all thy ways acknowledge Him, . . .
6. "Remember the sabbath day, . . .
7. "If the Son therefore shall make you free, . . .
8. "Call unto Me, and I will answer thee, . . .
9. "Blessed is the man that walketh not in the counsel of the ungodly, . . .
10. "So then every one of us . . .

1. . . . Thou anointest my head with oil; my cup runneth over" (Psalm 23. 5)
2. . . . and come short of the glory of God" (Romans 3. 23).
3. . . . that Christ Jesus came into the world to save sinners; of whom I am chief" (1 Timothy 1. 15).
4. . . . that whosoever believeth in Him should not perish, but have everlasting life" (John 3. 16).
5. . . . and He shall direct thy paths" (Proverbs 3. 6).
6. . . . to keep it holy" (Exodus 20. 8).
7. . . . ye shall be free indeed" (John 8. 36).
8. . . . and shew thee great and mighty things, which thou knowest not" (Jeremiah 33. 3).
9. . . . nor standeth in the way of sinners, nor sitteth in the seat of the scornful" (Psalm 1. 1).
10. . . . shall give account of himself to God" (Romans 14. 12).

Missionaries and Countries

CAN you correctly match each famous missionary with the country with which he is associated?

1. J. Hudson Taylor—India or China?
2. Robert Moffat—South Africa or Chile?
3. Wilfred Grenfell—Labrador or Arabia?
4. Adoniram Judson—New Zealand or Burma?
5. John G. Paton—New Hebrides or Alaska?
6. David Livingstone—Brazil or Africa?
7. Jonathan Goforth—China or Argentina?
8. James Gilmour—Mongolia or Japan?
9. Alexander Mackay—Panama or Africa?
10. William Carey—Borneo or India?

Answers

1. China.
2. South Africa.
3. Labrador.
4. Burma.
5. New Hebrides
6. Africa.
7. China.
8. Mongolia.
9. Africa.
10. India.

TAKE YOUR ? CHOICE

1. The sixth book of the New Testament is James, Galatians, Romans.
2. The oldest man of the Bible was Ahab, Solomon, Methuselah.
3. The first Christian martyr was Philip, Stephen, Andrew.
4. A son of Jacob was Nehemiah, Issachar, Nimrod.
5. Jesus raised the daughter of Jairus, Silas, Festus.
6. Paul did not write the book of Ephesians, Jude, Colossians.
7. Samson was captured by the Egyptians, Philistines, Romans.
8. The book in which we read the story of Joseph is Genesis, Exodus, Leviticus.
9. An island of the Mediterranean is Corinth, Macedonia, Cyprus.
10. The number of Psalms is seventy-five, one hundred, one hundred and fifty.

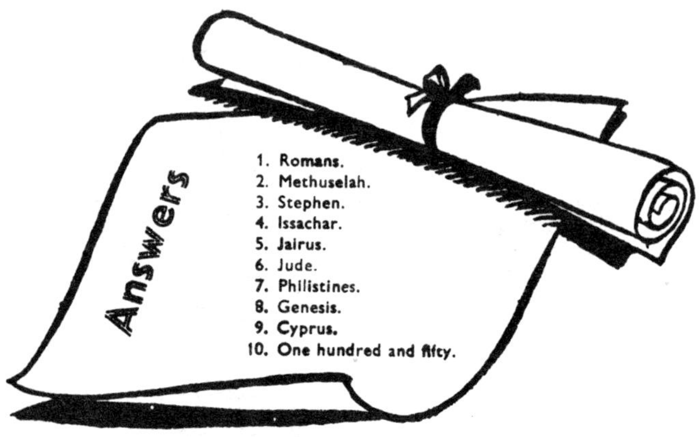

OCCUPATIONS

What was the occupation of each of these men?

1. PAUL.
2. CORNELIUS.
3. ADAM.
4. DAVID.
5. ANDREW.
6. MATTHEW.
7. FELIX.
8. LUKE.
9. NIMROD.
10. JOSEPH.

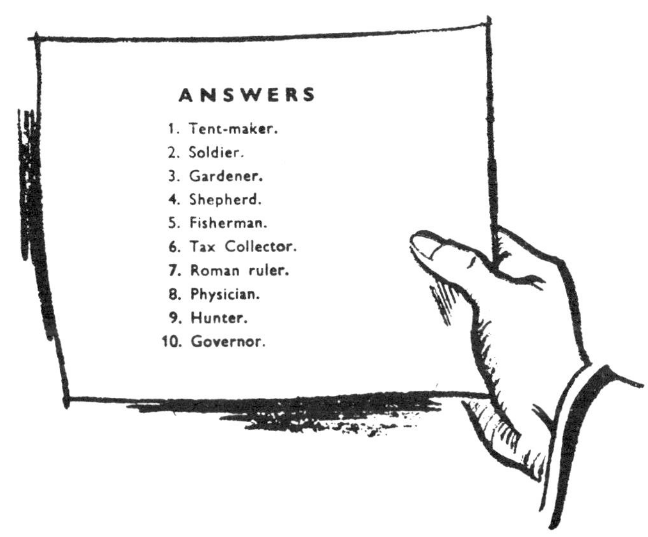
ANSWERS

1. Tent-maker.
2. Soldier.
3. Gardener.
4. Shepherd.
5. Fisherman.
6. Tax Collector.
7. Roman ruler.
8. Physician.
9. Hunter.
10. Governor.

BIBLE NAMES OF WOMEN

Here are ten sets of women's names. Which single name in each set is found in the Bible?

1.	SUSANNA,	CAROLYN,	HELEN.
2.	PEGGY,	RHODA,	ELSIE.
3.	PHOEBE,	JEAN,	DOROTHY.
4.	JENNY,	FLORENCE,	DORCAS.
5.	CLAUDIA,	LORETTA,	MARGARET.
6.	JUDITH,	RUBY,	MILDRED.
7.	AGNES,	SHIRLEY,	ANNA.
8.	MABEL,	BERNICE,	CAROL.
9.	EDNA,	JULIA,	PATRICIA.
10.	LOIS,	VIVIAN,	EDITH.

Answers

GENERAL QUIZ

1. What kind of food did Jacob's sons seek in Egypt?
2. Who were the Stoics?
3. Name two queens of the Bible.
4. Who was John Bunyan?
5. Which book occurs first in the New Testament—Jude or Philemon?
6. What did the Lord Jesus do for Jairus?
7. Name a Bible character who was lame.
8. Who asked, "Tell me, I pray thee, wherein thy great strength lieth, and wherewith thou mightest be bound to afflict thee"?
9. Who was Ahasuerus?
10. What New Testament Ruler's wife had a fearful dream?
11. Did Julius Caesar live before or after the birth of Christ?
12. Name a Bible character with just two letters in his name?
13. Name two Bible characters who were blind for brief periods.
14. Did David write more than five Psalms?
15. Who was Festus?

ANSWERS

1. Corn.
2. A philosophical sect mentioned in the book of Acts.
3. Vashti and Jezebel.
4. The author of Pilgrim's Progress.
5. Philemon.
6. He raised his daughter from the dead.
7. Mephibosheth.
8. Delilah.
9. Esther's husband and a king
10. Pilate.
11. Before.
12. Og, king of Bashan.
13. Samson and Paul.
14. Yes, many more.
15. A Roman ruler of Judaea

TRUE OR FALSE

1. The book of Matthew is longer than the book of Jude.
2. The name "George" is not mentioned in the Bible.
3. In the story of David and Goliath, David is wounded by the giant.
4. Martin Luther was born in Switzerland.
5. We read about Salome in the New Testament.
6. India is not mentioned in the Bible.
7. Galatians comes before Philippians.
8. The last word of the Bible is "Amen."
9. Pilate was a Greek.
10. Lois and Eunice were related.
11. Mirrors were unknown in Bible days.
12. Timothy was one of the twelve disciples.
13. Gad and Dan were sons of Jacob.
14. Miriam was the sister of Moses.
15. Earthquakes are not mentioned in the Bible.

ANSWERS

1. True.	8. True.
2. True.	9. False.
3. False.	10. True.
4. False.	11. False.
5. True.	12. False.
6. False.	13. True.
7. True.	14. True.

15 False.

UNFINISHED VERSES

1. "Blessed are the meek: . . .
2. "All we like sheep have gone astray; we have turned every one to his own way; . . .
3. "He restoreth my soul: . . .
4. "For I am not ashamed of the Gospel of Christ: . . .
5. "We love Him, . . .
6. "And we know that all things work together for good . . .
7. "Thou shalt not bear . . .
8. "And now abideth faith, hope, charity, these three; . .
9. "He that dwelleth in the secret place of the most High . . .
10. "If we confess our sins, He is faithful and just to forgive us our sins, . . .

Answers

1. . . . for they shall inherit the earth" (Matthew 5. 5.)
2. . . . and the Lord hath laid on Him the iniquity of us all" (Isaiah 53. 6).
3. . . . He leadeth me in the paths of righteousness for His name's sake" (Psalm 23. 3).
4. . . . for it is the power of God unto salvation to every one that believeth; to the Jew first, and also to the Greek" (Romans 1. 16).
5. . . . because He first loved us" (1 John 4. 19).
6. . . . to them that love God, to them who are the called according to His purpose" (Romans 8. 28).
7. . . . false witness against thy neighbour" (Exodus 20. 16).
8. . . . but the greatest of these is charity" (1 Cor. 13. 13).
9. . . . shall abide under the shadow of the Almighty" (Psalm 91. 1).
10. ...and to cleanse us from all unrighteousness" (1 John1 . 9)

Women of the Bible

How many of these Bible women can you identify from the first and last letters of their names?

1. E .... h
2. R .... h
3. H .... h
4. M .... m
5. J l
6. M .... y
7. D .... h
8. H .... r
9. R l
10. L .... s
11. N i
12. M .... a
13. E .... r
14. L .... h
15. E .... e
16. R .... h
17. S .... h
18. E .... e
19. P .... a
20. S .... a

ANSWERS

1. Elisabeth.
2. Ruth.
3. Hannah.
4. Miriam.
5. Jezebel.
6. Mary.
7. Deborah.
8. Hagar.
9. Rachel.
10. Lois.
11. Naomi.
12. Martha.
13. Esther.
14. Leah.
15. Eunice.
16. Rebekah.
17. Sarah.
18. Eve.
19. Priscilla.
20. Sapphira.

Missing Men

Two prominent men are missing from each group below. Can you name them?

THE SONS OF JACOB

Naphtali	Issachar	Dan	Zebulun
Asher	Reuben	Gad	Simeon
Levi	Judah		

THE DISCIPLES OF CHRIST

John	Peter	Judas	Simon
Bartholomew	Andrew	James	Thaddeus
Matthew	James		

CHARACTERS AND CLUES

CAN you identify each Bible character from the three clues? This quiz will make a lively contest between two groups. Give one side all odd numbered sets, and the other side all even numbered sets. Count one point for each clue that must be given before the character is identified. Naturally, it will be best to identify the character with just one or two clues, if possible. The side having the least number of points at the conclusion is the winner.

1

1. He was converted on the road to Damascus.
2. His original name was Saul.
3. He wrote many New Testament books!

2

1. He was a judge of Israel.
2. He was very strong.
3. Delilah was his wife!

3

1. She was the sister of Lazarus.
2. She lived in Bethany.
3. Her sister's name was Mary!

4

1. He committed a crime in Egypt.
2. Miriam was his sister.
3. He led the Children of Israel out of Egypt!

5

1. He wrote many of the Psalms.
2. He was a king of Israel.
3. He slew Goliath!

6

1. She was the daughter of Laban.
2. She was the sister of Leah.
3. Jacob was her husband!

7

1. He journeyed with Abraham.
2. Abraham was his uncle.
3. His wife turned into a pillar of salt!

8

1. He tried to slay David.
2. He consulted the witch of Endor.
3. He was a wicked king of Israel!

9

1. He was a Roman centurion.
2. He became a Christian.
3. He was baptized by Peter!

10

1. He had eleven brothers.
2. He had strange dreams.
3. He was cast into a pit!

11

1. This man's wife had a fearful dream.
2. He was a Roman ruler.
3. Christ appeared before him!

12

1. He wrote one New Testament book.
2. He was one of the twelve disciples.
3. John was his brother!

13

1. She became a queen.
2. Wicked Haman plotted against her people.
3. Mordecai was her guardian!

14

1. He was a leader of the Children of Israel.
2. He conquered Canaan.
3. He directed the fall of Jericho!

15

1. He had three sons.
2. One of them was named Shem.
3. He built a great boat!

16

1. She was a daughter of Laban.
2. She was "tender eyed."
3. Jacob was her husband!

17

1. His mother was named Lois.
2. He was a Christian worker.
3. Paul wrote two epistles to him!

18

1. She was a prophetess of the Children of Israel.
2. She complained against Moses.
3. Moses and Aaron were her brothers!

19

1. Jesus called him from his work to become a disciple.
2. He was a tax collector by trade.
3. He wrote one of the gospels!

20

1. She dedicated her son to the Lord.
2. Her husband was named Elkanah.
3. Samuel was her son!

21

1. He was a wicked ruler of New Testament Days.
2. He was the King of Judæa.
3. He ordered the slaying of many infants!

22

1. He was one of the twelve disciples.
2. He was slow to believe his Lord.
3. The Lord invited him to come close and prove that He had risen from the tomb!

23

1. He was the son of David.
2. He became a famous king.
3. He was very wise!

24

1. The Lord commanded him to preach at Nineveh.
2. His ship was caught in a great storm.
3. He was cast overboard!

25

1. She was the mother of Isaac.
2. She died at Hebron.
3. Abraham was her husband!

26

1. She was a Moabitish woman.
2. She went to Bethlehem with her mother-in-law.
3. Boaz became her husband!

27

1. He was once called Belteshazzar.
2. He would not eat the king's meat.
3. He interpreted Nebuchadnezzar's dream!

28

1. The Lord Jesus declared that He would abide at this man's house.
2. And the Lord was joyfully received.
3. This man climbed a sycamore tree!

29

1. He restored a widow's son to life.
2. He was once fed by ravens.
3. He ascended into heaven by a whirlwind!

30

1. This man had three "friends."
2. He lost all of his worldly goods.
3. He is noted for his patience!

31

1. He was a son of Isaac.
2. He was a twin.
3. Jacob was his brother!

32

1. She lived in the valley of Sorek.
2. She was in league with the Philistines.
3. She betrayed a strong man!

33

1. This man was stoned to death in the presence of Saul, who later became Paul.
2. He was a faithful worker for the Lord.
3. He was the first Christian martyr!

34

1. He was the son of King Saul.
2. His son was named Mephibosheth.
3. He was a dear friend of David!

35

1. He wrote the book of Acts.
2. He journeyed with the apostle Paul.
3. He also wrote one of the gospels!

36

1. He was a rich Jew at the time of Jesus' crucifixion.
2. He asked Pilate for the body of Jesus.
3. He buried the body of Jesus in a new tomb!

37

1. An angel told her that she had found favour with God.
2. Elisabeth was her cousin.
3. She sang a song of praise unto the Lord!

38

1. He "was a man sent from God."
2. He ate locusts and wild honey.
3. He preached in the wilderness of Judæa!

39

1. He was dedicated to the Lord when a child.
2. He was a great priest and prophet of the Children of Israel.
3. Hannah was his mother!

40

1. He was a son of Zebedee.
2. He was a fisherman by trade.
3. James was his brother!

41

1. He is first mentioned in the fourth chapter of Genesis.
2. He was a shepherd.
3. His brother became jealous of him!

42

1. He accompanied Paul and Barnabas on their missionary journeys.
2. He is sometimes called "John" in Scripture.
3. He wrote one of the gospels!

43

1. He lived in Bethany.
2. He was raised from the dead by Jesus.
3. He was the brother of Mary and Martha!

44

1. He was one of the twelve disciples.
2. He brought his brother to Jesus.
3. There are six letters in his name!

45

1. Her husband was named Zacharias.
2. Mary was her cousin.
3. John the Baptist was her son!

46

1. He was the son of Terah.
2. He founded the Hebrew nation.
3. He left his home in Ur of the Chaldees!

47

1. He was one of the Twelve disciples.
2. His home was in Bethsaida.
3. There are six letters in his name!

48

1. Two of this man's sons were Reuben and Judah.
2. He journeyed into Egypt.
3. Benjamin was his youngest son!

49

1. This dishonest man is mentioned in the book of Acts.
2. He kept back part of the money that belonged to the church.
3. His wife was named Sapphira!

50

1. He was a son of Sarah.
2. He was deceived by one of his sons.
3. Rebekah was his wife!

Answers

To Characters and Clues

1. Paul
2. Samson
3. Martha
4. Moses
5. David
6. Rachel
7. Lot
8. Saul
9. Cornelius
10. Joseph
11. Pilate
12. James
13. Esther
14. Joshua
15. Noah
16. Leah
17. Timothy
18. Miriam
19. Matthew
20. Hannah
21. Herod
22. Thomas
23. Solomon
24. Jonah
25. Sarah
26. Ruth
27. Daniel
28. Zacchæus
29. Elijah
30. Job
31. Esau
32. Delilah
33. Stephen
34. Jonathan
35. Luke
36. Joseph of Arimathæa
37. Mary
38. John the Baptist
39. Samuel
40. John
41. Abel
42. Mark
43. Lazarus
44. Andrew
45. Elisabeth
46. Abraham
47. Philip
48. Jacob
49. Ananias
50. Isaac

BIBLE SPELLING BEE

Here is a list of names that may be used for a lively spell-down contest.

1. Canaan
2. Elijah
3. Obadiah
4. Damascus
5. Gamaliel
6. Deborah
7. Judah
8. Isaiah
9. Deuteronomy
10. Malachi
11. Salome
12. Jericho
13. Demetrius
14. Jeremiah
15. Reuben
16. Philemon
17. Zechariah
18. Samaria
19. Hannah
20. Galilee
21. Nebuchadnezzar
22. Nehemiah
23. Mediterranean
24. Cornelius
25. Colossians
26. Rhoda
27. Ezekiel
28. Antioch
29. Nazareth
30. Israel
31. Obadiah
32. Lazarus
33. Sapphira
34. Priscilla
35. Revelation
36. Pharaoh
37. Ecclesiastes
38. Philistine
39. Tarsus
40. Bartholomew
41. Philippians
42. Delilah
43. Ethiopia
44. Methuselah
45. Solomon
46. Esau
47. Ishmael
48. Ananias
49. Thessalonians
50. Nicodemus
51. Japheth
52. Aaron
53. Gideon
54. Pharisee
55. Galatians
56. Jerusalem
57. Jezebel
58. Chloe
59. Chronicles
60. Gethsemane
61. Leviticus
62. Phœnicia
63. Hagar
64. Berea
65. Malachi
66. Zacchæus
67. Armenia
68. Haggai
69. Ephesians
70. Enoch
71. Sinai
72. Cæsar
73. Levi
74. Goliath
75. Cyprus
76. Magdalene
77. Tyre
78. Crete
79. Mesopotamia
80. Macedonia
81. Naphtali
82. Patriarch
83. Tiberias
84. Belshazzar
85. Elisha
86. Synagogue
87. Naomi
88. Balaam
89. Orpah
90. Nineveh
91. Onesimus
92. Darius
93. Syracuse
94. Ararat
95. Zebedee
96. Cæsarea
97. Capernaum
98. Babylonia
99. Smyrna
100. Ephraim